I just feel...

A 31-Day Devotional for Healing the Emotions

Rebekah McLeod

MARIGOLD PRESS BOOKS

A Division of International School of Story

Copyright © 2023 Rebekah McLeod. *First Edition.*

All rights reserved. No portion of this book may be reproduced, stored in a retrieval system, or transmitted in any form or by any means–electronic, mechanical, photocopy, recording, scanning, or other–except for brief quotations in critical reviews or articles, without the prior written permission of the author.

Published in Savannah, Georgia by Marigold Press Books, a division of International School of Story.

Marigold Press Books titles may be purchased in bulk for educational, business, fund-raising, or sales promotional use. For information, please email marigoldpressbooks@gmail.com.

Fonts and stock images licensed for commercial use.

All Scripture quotations, unless otherwise indicated, are taken from the Holy Bible, New International Version®, NIV®. Copyright ©1973, 1978, 1984, 2011 by Biblica, Inc.™ Used by permission of Zondervan. All rights reserved worldwide. www.zondervan.com. The "NIV" and "New International Version" are trademarks registered in the United States Patent and Trademark Office by Biblica, Inc.™

Scripture quotations marked (NLT) are taken from the Holy Bible, New Living Translation, copyright ©1996, 2004, 2015 by Tyndale House Foundation. Used by permission of Tyndale House Publishers, Carol Stream, Illinois 60188. All rights reserved.

Scripture quotations marked "NKJV" are taken from the New King James Version. Copyright © 1982 by Thomas Nelson, Inc. Used by permission. All rights reserved. Bible text from the New King James Version® is not to be reproduced in copies or otherwise by any means except as permitted in writing by Thomas Nelson, Inc., Attn: Bible Rights and Permissions, P.O. Box 141000, Nashville, TN 37214-1000. http://www.nelsonbibles.com/

Scripture quotations marked "MSG" or "The Message" are taken from The Message. Copyright 1993, 1994, 1995, 1996, 2000, 2001, 2002. Used by permission of NavPress Publishing Group. http://www.navpress.com/

Scripture quotations marked "TPT" are from The Passion Translation®. Copyright © 2017, 2018, 2020 by Passion & Fire Ministries, Inc. Used by permission. All rights reserved. ThePassionTranslation.com.

Scripture quotations marked "KJV" are taken from the Holy Bible, King James Version (Public Domain).

Scripture quotations marked (CEV) are from the Contemporary English Version Copyright © 1991, 1992, 1995 by American Bible Society. Used by Permission.

Scripture quotations are from the ESV® Bible (The Holy Bible, English Standard Version®), © 2001 by Crossway, a publishing ministry of Good News Publishers. Used by permission. All rights reserved. The ESV text may not be quoted in any publication made available to the public by a Creative Commons license. The ESV may not be translated in whole or in part into any other language.

Scripture quotations marked (GNT) are from the Good News Translation in Today's English Version- Second Edition Copyright © 1992 by American Bible Society. Used by Permission.

Scripture quotations marked HCSB are taken from the Holman Christian Standard Bible®, Used by Permission HCSB ©1999,2000,2002,2003,2009 Holman Bible Publishers. Holman Christian Standard Bible®, Holman CSB®, and HCSB® are federally registered trademarks of Holman Bible Publishers.

Scripture quotations marked "NASB" are taken from the New American Standard Bible®, Copyright © 1960, 1962, 1963, 1968, 1971, 1972, 1973, 1975, 1977, 1995 by The Lockman Foundation. Used by permission. www.Lockman.org

All Scripture marked with the designation "GW" is taken from GOD'S WORD®. © 1995, 2003, 2013, 2014, 2019, 2020 by God's Word to the Nations Mission Society. Used by permission.

Scripture taken from the Holy Bible: International Standard Version©. Copyright © 1996-2012 by The ISV Foundation. ALL RIGHTS RESERVED INTERNATIONALLY. Used by permission.

Scripture quotations marked CSB have been taken from the Christian Standard Bible®, Copyright © 2017 by Holman Bible Publishers. Used by permission. Christian Standard Bible® and CSB® are federally registered trademarks of Holman Bible Publishers.

Rebekah McLeod, *I Just Feel: A 31-Day Devotional to Heal the Emotions*, https://www.rebekahmcleod.com/

ISBN 978-1-942923-65-7 | Library of Congress Control Number: 2023917582

Cover Design: Skye McLeod

Printed in the United States of America

To Emma

For showing me what it looks like to follow Jesus and serve others wholeheartedly. You are a treasure!

CONTENTS
I just feel...

Introduction 1

DAY 1: Like I'll Never Be Loved the Way I Want to be Loved 5

DAY 2: Like I Never Finish What I Start 9

DAY 3: Fat 11

DAY 4: Like Nothing I Do Matters 15

DAY 5: Like a Bad Parent 19

DAY 6: Like My Heart Will Never Recover From This Hurt 23

DAY 7: Anxious. 27

DAY 8: Like I'm Way Off Track Because of My Own Poor Choices 29

DAY 9: Insecure (Full of Self-Doubt) 31

DAY 10: Confused About This Decision. 33

DAY 11: Exhausted by the Needs of Others. 35

DAY 12: Frustrated With My Marraige 37

DAY 13: Like Everyone Else Has It Together and I'm a Hot Mess. 41

CONTENTS (cont.)

I just feel...

DAY 14: Lonely................................ 43

DAY 15: Unappreciated 45

DAY 16: Like Time is Running Out 47

DAY 17: Like I Can't Forgive Them for What They've Done.................................. 49

DAY 18: Guilty for Spending/Eating/Drinking Too Much 53

DAY 19: Too Lazy to Pray 55

DAY 20: Like I Care Too Much About What Other People Think 57

DAY 21: Depressed 59

DAY 22: Like My Mind is Spinning 61

DAY 23: Jealous 63

DAY 24: Tired of Waiting for Things to Change ... 65

DAY 25: Rejected 67

DAY 26: Trapped 69

DAY 27: Like Nothing Good Can Come Out of This Situation 71

DAY 28: Overwhelmed With Lust for Something/
Someone I Can't Have 73

DAY 29: Disillusioned With the Church 75

DAY 30: Discontented 77

DAY 31: Sickened by the Injustice in the World . . . 79

About the Author 83

I just feel...

A 31-Day Devotional for Healing the Emotions

Rebekah McLeod

Introduction

I don't know about you, but my mind is sometimes assaulted with self-deprecating messages. Those in the medical camp—the psychologists and psychiatrists—might suggest these come from childhood experiences, trauma or possibly a mood disorder or other psychiatric condition. In the education camp, personality theorists say it's our genetic wiring that determines whether we are prone to emotional dysregulation or feelings of low self-esteem. Pastors and priests in the spiritual camp tell us these messages of shame come directly from the Enemy of our souls, Satan, as he attempts to steal our joy and discourage our forward progress.

I do not claim to be an expert in medicine, education or theology, but I do know we are three-part beings; body, soul and spirit. Is it not beyond the realm of belief to think that in our human complexity, all three of the above mentioned theories could contain a morsel of truth? Some of us grew up in homes where shameful put-downs were considered a normal part of parenting; some of us are more prone, based on our personalities, to view the world through the lens of feeling rather than thought; and some of us—especially the spiritually sensitive types—are assaulted by dark forces as they live out their purpose on Earth.

Regardless of why we struggle with these negative feelings, we know they exist and have a destructive influence in our lives, causing us to give into self-doubt, depression and even despair. Sometimes we wake up and feel as if a fog of discouragement has descended over us; we may not be able to discern the thoughts behind our emotions; we are only aware of feeling sad or lonely or anxious.

I have learned that the only way to deal with these emotions is to actively refute them (sometimes out loud) with truth.

I wrote this devotional during a time when I was feeling lost in my own life; I was grieving for my daughter, who had recently lost her husband to suicide; I was also struggling with knowing what direction to take in my work. It was a time of sadness and uncertainty when many negative feelings surfaced, and I found myself running to the Bible's truths as a lifeline to keep myself from falling into despair.

If you are in a season of grief, confusion or doubt and you find anxiety and depression knocking on your door, I pray these writings will bring comfort to your heart and mind. As Christians, we have been given a wealth of promises to lean into when our emotions seem to betray us; and remember, emotions come and go like waves on the ocean. They are temporary, and if we hold onto truth, we will make it through. The fog will lift.

I wrote these in the same style as the popular devotional, *Jesus Calling* by Sarah Young, which has been a comfort to me and to millions of other Christ followers around the world. Each day I present a feeling I have struggled with (or am currently struggling with) and the truth I believe our loving God would speak to it.

May the truths of His Word and His Spirit bring comfort and healing to our minds and emotions!

DAY 1

I just feel...

LIKE I'LL NEVER BE LOVED THE WAY I WANT TO BE LOVED

My Child,

There are empty spaces in your soul from your childhood; places your parents were not able to fill because of their own wounds, sin and unwillingness to receive My love. Films, TV and the media at large tells you there is a special person out there who will say and do everything right so that the emptiness in your heart will finally be filled. Other messengers tell you that your current spouse is the wrong one, and if you could just divorce him/her and continue the search, you will be better off in the long run.

The truth is, all human love is fallible. Human hearts are hungry and needy, and so often the love humans give and receive is more manipulative than pure and unconditional.

I am the only source of true, unconditional love. There is no other love like Mine, which is shed abroad in your heart through the Holy Spirit. It is this perfect love that quells all the longings of your body, soul and spirit. When you are in the presence of My love, notice that you feel no hunger, thirst or any other need—your being becomes caught up in love.

It pains My heart to see My children running after substitute love; love which will never provide the interior rest and satisfaction My love can give.

As soon as you surrender your search for incomplete love, I am waiting to enfold you in the wholeness and security of My divine love. I am not unaware of your need for companionship, but I know your human relationships will be compromised as long as your deepest need for love is not met in Me.

Come to Me and let Me lavish you with my extravagant love! You are my delight, and it is My pleasure to give you the Kingdom.

There is no *fear* in love. But *perfect love* drives out fear, because fear has to do with punishment...

1 John 4:18 NIV

Look with wonder at the *depth* of the Father's *marvelous* love that He has *lavished* on us! He has called us and made us his very own *beloved* children.

1 John 3:1 TPT

DAY 2

I just feel...

LIKE I NEVER FINISH WHAT I START

My Child,

What was to be done has been done. You may think that you drop things randomly, but there is an order to my creative purposes, and those projects you think you should have completed were not meant to be completed. I have brought you to this point in your life by my perfect divine purpose. When you receive your instructions from my Spirit, the things I planned for you to accomplish are completed in time.

I have things for you to do, my child, and those things will be completed as you walk in step with my Spirit. Trust me to give you the right assignments at the right time. If you go out trying to find your own assignments, you will become more frustrated. Do not compare your assignment with anyone else's. I made you just as you are for my exact purposes! The things you consider a liability, I see as a design strength. Your combination of personality, gifts, strengths and weaknesses make you exactly suited to the needs of my Kingdom. Do not look back at what you think you should have done, look ahead at how I will use you to impact those I love. You are perfectly suited to complete the work I have for you to do. Rest in my wisdom.

―――

For we are God's handiwork, created in Christ Jesus to do good works, which God prepared in advance for us to do.

Ephesians 2:10 NIV

But one thing I do: Forgetting what is behind and straining toward what is ahead, I press on toward the goal to win the prize for which God has called me heavenward in Christ Jesus.

Philippians 3:13-14 NIV

DAY 3

I just feel...

FAT

My Child,

Your body is miraculous. I made your body so complex, and if you only knew all your body does in a day, you would marvel at its workings! Think about how much your body is capable of, besides just being a number on a scale or a measuring tape. Your brain holds trillions of synapses, a thousand times the number of stars in the galaxy. Your blood produces 17 million new cells a day; your eyes can process 36,000 pieces of information in a single hour; your skin completely regenerates itself every 28 days. The wonders are endless!

Your bones, height, and body frame have been influenced by many factors outside of your control. You were born with a certain composition, hormone structure, and many things that affect your body today continue to be outside of your control.

Stop fighting to change what I never asked you to change, my child.

When you see yourself in the mirror, you are tempted to compare yourself with others and to focus on what you consider to be imperfections. Focus instead on all the ways your body is a source of generosity and life and love!

You live in a world that judges by what it sees, but what is unseen is so much more important. I have given you a mind that can choose what it thinks, just as you can choose what clothes to wear in the morning. Will you choose to think condemning thoughts about your body or will you hear Me blessing your body as it is? I love your body. Your body is beautiful in form, functional in design, and a thing to be celebrated! My children have hated their bodies for too long.

Your body is my crowning achievement in creation. It's no wonder Satan has so violently waged war against it. Please, my child, do not join him in his exploits. Receive my complete and total approval of your body. You are my beloved, in whom I am well pleased. You do not need to lose weight to be acceptable to me.

Stop thinking that when there is less of you in the room, there will be more of you to give the world.

You are perfect *just as you are*. Health will come to your body in direct proportion as your mind is renewed in my love. Breathe into your lungs the complete worthiness I have given you as a physical being on my Earth. You are fiercely loved. You are worth fighting for. Your body is being used in the scope of my divine purposes day by day.

You, my child, are captivating in every way!

I praise you because I am fearfully and wonderfully made.
Psalm 139:14 NIV

And be renewed in the spirit of your mind.
Ephesians 4:23 KJV

DAY 4

I just feel...

LIKE NOTHING I DO MATTERS

My Child,

My economy is not the world's economy. The system of the world relies on money, power and status to measure success. When you place yourself on that scale, you will always come up short. Even those who gain some measure of worldly success are at risk of falling into despair within that system. My Kingdom is upside down. The only commodity in my Kingdom is love. Every act of love, regardless of how small it may seem, has great impact. Imagine a magnificent quilt in the works, made of rich, colorful fabric squares; each act of love is a carefully sewn stitch. You think the work you do is invisible, but it is not! Each small act of kindness is advancing my Kingdom in the world! Every child's tears you dry, every crumb you sweep off the floor, every hot meal you put on the table—you are building my Kingdom.

I may have called you into the workplace to perform a role in business or in health care, or you may find yourself at home with children or unemployed and waiting for your next assignment. Regardless of where you find yourself, your first priority is to love. Love matters above all other human activity. The world system values productivity, the bottom line, and being right above relationship; but my children know better.

Your life is on display, and you cannot know the impact of your life at any given moment. You don't see it, but many people around you draw strength and encouragement from your being. At every moment of your existence, the heavenly hosts are cheering you on, and I am singing over you with delight.

Do not give an audience to the dark voices who tell you your life is meaningless. These are lies and you must refute them with the truth, my child. You must stand up in your identity! Your life is eternally valuable, regardless of what you are producing. Think of a baby and how adored that child is in the family—an infant who does nothing but cry and eat and demand attention! Your value is not tied to your performance. You have been given my name, my seal, my inheritance. Walk in your dignity, child of God!

For the Lord takes *delight* in his people; He crowns the humble with *victory*.

Psalm 149:4 NIV

When you believed, you were *marked* in him with a seal, the *promised* Holy Spirit…

Ephesians 1:13 NIV

DAY 5

I just feel...

LIKE A BAD PARENT

My Child,

Your children are ultimately not a reflection of you; they are a reflection of Me. Your children have been birthed into the world for a purpose, and I have given them to you in order that you might learn how to love as I love. I understand your humanity, and I know you will sometimes struggle to receive my love and to give it to your children. And sometimes, when you think you're getting it right, your children will be unable or unwilling to receive it.

Consider the parable of the prodigal son: a loving father has two sons, neither of whom know how to receive the father's love. The prodigal values the lesser god of pleasure and the elder brother chooses performance and right living to try to earn his father's favor. Both sons have full access to their loving father's inheritance, and yet both refuse it.

My love is not based on performance. My love is granted based on who I am, and my children do not have to earn my acceptance.

Silence the shaming voices telling you how to perform as a parent. Open your eyes to see the endless, creative ways my Spirit can lead you to love, instruct, discipline, encourage and nurture your child's heart. You will never be a perfect parent, but you are the perfect parent for the children I gave you!

I exist outside of time, and I can see the entire breadth of your child's life. You cannot know the plans I have, but trust me that I have your child's life in my hands. Your vision is limited, but mine is not.

Refuse to be overwhelmed by the daily tasks of parenting. Breathe. I have given you one day's worth of mercies at a time; do not look too far ahead or you will grow weary. Bring me your burdens, moment by moment, receive my peace and be refreshed in my love. I am so proud of you, my child!

Do not be anxious about anything, but in every situation, by prayer and petition, with thanksgiving, present your requests to

God. And the peace of God, which surpasses all understanding, will guard your heart and mind in Christ Jesus.

Philippians 4:6-7 NIV

He made from one blood all nations who live on the earth. He set the times and places where they should live.

Acts 17:26 NLT

DAY 6

I just feel...

LIKE MY HEART WILL NEVER RECOVER FROM THIS HURT

My Child,

I see your pain. I have never abandoned you, not for one second, even though you have felt alone at times. I promise that I am filtering every experience in your life through my hands of love. Wounds of the heart take heaping amounts of time, compassion and community to heal. You may feel more safe in isolating yourself, but this is a time to allow people to love you. Take comfort in those I have sent to help you in your time of healing.

I understand your anger, frustration and your need to understand why. I am able to handle your most difficult questions and your darkest emotions. Bring them to me and do not condemn yourself for the way your mind and soul wrestle against the wrongs that have been done. You have so many forces coming against you, my child, but my power is still greater than any negative force within or without! I will help you process and overcome the pain you have endured, and none of your suffering will be wasted.

I know it is difficult to believe I am still good when you have been hurt. It feels unfair and it seems that I am unconcerned for your well-being. Nothing could be further from the truth. I am continually bringing you further along in my redemptive plan for your life. You don't see it now, but it is a beautiful sight to behold!

I give rest to my beloved—more rest than you often give yourself permission to take. I alone know exactly how and when this pain will be resolved in your life. Do not fall into the trap of numbing yourself or busying yourself to avoid your feelings. Be open to sharing your heart with safe people, and in time you will move past your hurt. I am doing my finest work in you right now, my child! You are not failing a test or falling short or being weak—you are shedding old skin and growing into a new person of depth, compassion and faith.

The Lord is close to the brokenhearted, and he rescues those whose spirits are crushed.

Psalm 34:18 NLT

And the God of all grace, who called you to his eternal glory in Christ, after you have suffered a little while, will himself restore you and make you strong, firm and steadfast.

1 Pet 5:10 NIV

DAY 7

I just feel...

ANXIOUS

My Child,

You do not have to handle your life alone. You do not have to figure it all out. I have given you all the resources of heaven for every moment of your existence, and they reside inside you! My Spirit is ever-present to help you when you run into the many cares and worries that life brings. You don't have to earn or deserve this help—it is free and it is not given out based on your behavior.

There are many voices to silence if you are to enjoy my peace. You must actively guard the gates of your eyes and ears in order to cultivate a restful mind, and I will show you what to allow in and what to reject. Your sensitivity is not a liability or a weakness—it is a gift to be cherished!

I understand your fears about the future, your health, your family and your finances. I am not angry at you for worrying. I see your heart and I see exactly what triggers you to fear. Some of these triggers you can control and some you cannot. Receive My love and approval over the entirety of your being!

Open your hands to My sovereignty. Trust that whatever I allow to happen will be for your ultimate good. Do not give in to the temptation to look too far ahead. When you find your anxiety growing, close your eyes, place your hand on your chest and say, "Holy Spirit, come." I am right here, and I will come to you when you call on me.

Just as you hold a baby and soothe its fears, so I long to hold you and comfort you, my child. I love you with an everlasting love. Let your fears be drowned out by my presence.

Give all your worries and cares to God, for he cares about you.
1 Peter 5:7 NLT

That's why we can be so sure that every detail in our lives of love for God is worked into something good.
Romans 8:28 MSG

DAY 8

I just feel...

LIKE I'M WAY OFF TRACK BECAUSE OF MY OWN POOR CHOICES

My Child,

My perspective is so much broader than yours. Your life is a series of lessons, and I have made you in such a way that failure is a necessary part of the learning process. Remember when you learned to ride a bike? You had to fall many times before you were able to enjoy riding. I knew exactly how many times you would fall, and I was not disappointed when you failed. I knew each time you fell, you were one step closer to riding.

In the same way, those areas in your life where you feel you have fallen off track, I celebrate the fact that you are one less failure away from learning the lesson.

Do not lose heart in the process. Some lessons take years, even decades, to learn, and I am not in a rush.

The biggest temptation you will face as you learn and grow is to compare your life with others. Do not despair when you see others prospering in the very areas where you struggle. You have no idea where they started or where they will finish. My curriculum for my children is unique to each one, and you will do best to keep your eyes on the Teacher while you are learning.

There is no human choice that can outrun the reach of my grace. You may think your choices have destroyed your ability to recover, but I am in the business of resurrecting dead things. I never stop believing in you. I will do the impossible on your behalf as you trust in my redemptive power.

We do this by keeping our eyes on Jesus, the champion who initiates and perfects our faith.

Hebrews 12:2 NLT

There has never been the slightest doubt in my mind that the God who started this great work in you would keep at it and bring it to a flourishing finish on the very day Christ Jesus appears.

Philippians 1:6 MSG

DAY 9

I just feel...

INSECURE (FULL OF SELF-DOUBT)

My Child,

You have been through many experiences in life where you felt you had to figure things out yourself. In these times I was right there with you, but you distanced yourself from Me out of fear and the desire to protect yourself. Many of my children fall into the trap of self-sufficiency, which in the end is crushing. You were never meant to rely on yourself—I made you for intimacy with me.

There are two forms of self-sufficiency—the boasting kind and the insecure kind. Both forms distance you from the wide open space of my loving presence and push you into a place of fear.

I have called you, My child, and I have enabled you to do the work in front of you. Do not look to the right or to the left when stepping out into a new endeavor; trust that

I am sufficient to provide you with what you need. Your lack is my supply. I want you to be aware of your need for Me, but I do not want you beating yourself up for your shortcomings. Your security is not in your appearance or in your money or in your earthly relationships. Your security is found only in your identity as My child.

You do not need the approval of man to do what I have asked you to do. When you face criticism, slander and rejection, you do not have to allow it to devastate you. I will strengthen your spirit to continue moving forward while all the doubting voices assail you. As you become increasingly more grounded in my unconditional love and approval of you, you will grow sturdy and strong like an oak tree. You will provide shade and solace to others who are learning to trust in my love.

You're a tree replanted in Eden, bearing fresh fruit every month, never dropping a leaf, always in blossom.

Psalm 1:3 MSG

I am the vine, and you are the branches. If you stay joined to me, and I stay joined to you, then you will produce lots of fruit. But you cannot do anything without me.

John 15:5 CEV

DAY 10

I just feel...

CONFUSED ABOUT THIS DECISION

My Child,

You have been conditioned to mistrust your own heart. You are so afraid of making the wrong choice that you become paralyzed. Release the internal pressure you feel around making this decision. I have given you the power of choice that you might learn to walk in wisdom. You will make mistakes, and I have already covered them with my grace.

Instead of collecting opinions on which direction to go, get alone to a quiet place and connect with Me. I am waiting to help you, and you don't need to fear My disapproval. I have given you desires and My timing for their fulfillment is perfect. I promise I am not withholding anything good from you.

Refuse to overanalyze; surrender your need to control the outcome. You cannot know how this decision will play out, and it is not your job to avoid every risk. Where I ask you to step out, step out. If you step out and realize I have not asked you, step back. Do not beat yourself up for making a mistake. This is a process, and I am a patient teacher. You are learning to walk in step with Me, and when we are in sync, you will have a peaceful knowing deep down in your soul.

Since we live by the Spirit, let us keep in step with the Spirit.
Galatians 5:25 NIV

For God is not a God of confusion, but of peace.
1 Corinthians 14:33 ESV

DAY 11

I just feel...

EXHAUSTED BY THE NEEDS OF OTHERS

My Child,

I have made you in My image, as a giver of life. You strengthen and nourish those you love through your many acts of generosity. I understand you are in a season where you feel you are being stretched beyond your capacity to give. Call on me in your most overwhelmed moments, and I will steady you.

It is good to ask for help, My child. It is good to rest when you are in an intense season of giving. I never meant for you to carry all of these burdens alone. Humble yourself and allow others in your circle the gift of serving you so you can recharge.

Do not be afraid to say "no" in this season. Guard the treasures of your time and energy with great intention; only take on new activities if they feed your soul.

There is not a crack or crevice in your life that my love cannot fill. I never condemn you for feeling burned out, depressed or angry. I come closer to you in these times to comfort and reassure you; I send angels to minister to you as you rest.

So let's not get tired of doing what is good. At just the right time we will reap a harvest of blessing if we don't give up.

Galatians 6:9 NLT

He will order his angels to protect you wherever you go.

Psalm 91:11 NLT

DAY 12

I just feel...

FRUSTRATED WITH MY MARRIAGE

My Child,

Much is at stake in your marriage; much more than you can see with your human eyes. There are things I have for you to accomplish that you will only accomplish together with your spouse. Your destinies are now intricately woven together, and there are spiritual forces trying to tear down what I am building in your family.

I brought you two together for my purposes. Lift your eyes and gain a higher perspective. Your marriage is not only a channel for me to meet your needs; it is a channel for me to build my Kingdom. I am accomplishing so much more than you know through your union.

Do not give place to the Enemy of your soul, who would try to pit you against your spouse. Your marriage is an outpost of the gospel; it is the perfect training ground to master the arts of mercy, forgiveness and unconditional love. I have given you to one another that you might grow up in grace.

Your satisfaction is directly related to your trust in Me. It is an exercise in futility to manipulate your spouse to get your needs met. I am the source of all you need, and I will supply you with every good thing.

Do not give place to criticism, harsh words or bickering in your marriage. Where there has been hurt, come together and speak honestly and humbly, giving and receiving forgiveness. Express gratitude daily to one another; remember you are brothers and sisters in Christ, and as such you are to build one another up in the faith.

"Therefore, what God has joined together, let no one separate."
Mark 10:9 NIV

"Where do all the fights and quarrels among you come from? They come from your desires for pleasure, which are constantly fighting within you."
James 4:1 GNT

But *encourage* one another *daily*, as long as it is called 'Today,' so that none of you will be deceived by sin and *hardened* against God.

Hebrews 3:13 NLT

DAY 13

I just feel...

LIKE EVERYONE ELSE HAS IT TOGETHER AND I'M A HOT MESS

My Child,

I love every part of you, even the parts you think are messy. I have not asked you to keep up with, compete or outdo anyone else; I have only asked you to live each day in simple, childlike faith. Let all the burdensome expectations go; let the plates you've been spinning fall.

You will be surprised at how simple life can be when you focus only on the few things I have called you to do.

Walking in grace means you have My full permission to be your truest self. I am pleased when you allow others to see your vulnerability. When you do this, you unknowingly give others permission to be their honest selves as well. I yearn for you to understand that your value to Me is completely unrelated to your appearance, behavior or accomplishments. You are worth giving everything I have because I created you; you bear my name and I am a doting father!

Do not fall into the trap of looking to the world to validate you. The game is endless and the rules continually change. Step off the treadmill of insecurity and burnout. I came to rescue you from this cycle; My way is the way of peace and self-acceptance.

Jesus told them, 'This is the only work God wants from you: Believe in the one he has sent'.

John 6:29 NLT

Readily recognize what [God] wants from you, and quickly respond to it. Unlike the culture around you, always dragging you down to its level of immaturity, God brings the best out of you, develops well-formed maturity in you.

Romans 12:2 MSG

DAY 14

I just feel...

LONELY

My Child,

I have made your heart for deep connection and communion. The pain and emptiness you feel is a necessary warning sign that your relational life needs attention. Bring your pain to me and I will comfort you. There is nothing wrong with you; do not judge yourself as being weak or too needy. Just as the weather changes with the seasons, so have I ordained seasons of solitude for you that you might know me better alongside seasons of deep friendship with other people. I invite you to trust Me fully with your relational needs, as I know exactly what makes your heart come alive!

I see the deep pain you suffer when friends are lost, through broken fellowship or moves or even death. The times you cherish with close friends, sitting around the table, laughing and telling stories, are just a foretaste of the rich intimacy you will experience in my eternal Kingdom. Your heart is longing for reunion with Me, and that day is coming, My child!

Keep your spiritual eyes open for opportunities to build new relationships. I am always at work behind the scenes, creating connections between my children. Even now, I am sending reinforcements to you, that you might be encouraged and strengthened in your faith.

Be willing to be uncomfortable as you pursue relationships. Take a step out and I will meet you in surprising ways. Do not allow previous rejections to keep you from trying again. Your heart is safe with Me.

Behold, I stand at the door and knock. If anyone hears my voice and opens the door, I will come in to him and eat with him, and he with me.

Revelation 3:20 ESV

After David had finished talking with Saul, Jonathan became one in spirit with David, and he loved him as himself.

1 Samuel 18:1 NIV

DAY 15

I just feel...

UNAPPRECIATED

My Child,

The work you are doing is reaping eternal rewards. There are earthly rewards, which are temporary, and there are eternal rewards, which last forever. You may feel invisible doing the hundreds of everyday tasks that go unappreciated, but remember, your life is on display before My loving eyes. I see every single thing you do behind the scenes to make life easier for others.

When you feel discouraged, simply ask Me to send you an appreciation and I will do it! I have all the resources of heaven at my disposal, and I will send you just what you need to keep going.

Do not look to the right or left when you are feeling unappreciated. This is an open door for resentment and jealousy, and I want your mind and heart to be aligned as you do the work I have called you to do.

I have called you to be a channel of blessing in your sphere of influence, and your reward is coming. You are celebrated with great rejoicing in the spiritual realm!

―

Let your eyes look straight ahead; fix your gaze directly before you. Give careful thought to the paths for your feet and be steadfast in all your ways. Do not turn to the right or the left; keep your foot from evil.

Proverbs 4:25-26 NIV

DAY 16

I just feel...

LIKE TIME IS RUNNING OUT

My Child,

I am a God of more than enough. Feelings of panic and pressure are not from Me. Imagine yourself as a priceless piece of pottery; the longer I work on you, the more uniquely beautiful you become. With each year that passes, you are able to display more and more of my creative prowess!

My desire is that you would be content in the season you are in, and yet remain open to where I might lead you next. I am not in a rush, and you are not missing out. Do the work in front of you and be patient as I work behind the scenes to open doors of opportunity for you.

Surrender your desire to control the outcome of your life. When you walk in step with My Spirit, you will create ripples of impact far beyond your human ability. Set aside self-promotion; I will promote you when I know you are ready. Your life is constantly displaying My glory. Carry the flame of My love everywhere you go, and the deep meaning in life you are so longing for will be found.

So humble yourselves under the mighty power of God, and at the right time he will lift you up in honor.

1 Peter 5:6 NLT

But now, O Lord, you are our father; we are the clay, and you our potter; and we all are the work of your hand.

Isaiah 64:8 ESV

DAY 17

I just feel...

LIKE I CAN'T FORGIVE THEM FOR WHAT THEY'VE DONE

My Child,

Imagine yourself in a long corridor with many rooms, each door bearing the name of someone who has hurt you deeply. Imagine you walk past each door and you notice a pile of papers in the middle of each room, some piles larger than others. Now imagine Me walking with you to a door marked "Self" and me opening the door; inside is a pile of paper stacked up almost to the ceiling. You wonder how that paper got there. I show you a vision of yourself as a small child walking in with a pad of paper and writing the word, "BAD," and tearing it and throwing it on the pile.

Over and over as you grew, you continued walking into the room, writing down other condemning words, UGLY,

STUPID, NOT GOOD ENOUGH, each time adding more accusations to the pile.

Now imagine you can see a 3D image of the building, and you notice that the pile in the room marked SELF is at least five times higher than any of the other rooms in the building.

Yes, I want you to forgive others. But first, My child, you must forgive yourself. You have spent many years judging and condemning yourself for all kinds of things for which I have never condemned you.

Shame says that everything is ultimately your fault. My grace says you are released from every charge brought against you.

In fact, I want to burn down that whole building.

Let me show you how much I love you, that you might then be able to love yourself aright and then love others as well. Forgiveness cannot be given unless it is first received. I have come that you might walk unashamed and unhindered by condemnation.

Therefore, no condemnation now exists for those in Christ Jesus.

Romans 8:1 HCSB

He does not punish us for all our sins; he does not deal harshly with us, as we deserve. For his unfailing love toward those who fear him is as great as the height of the heavens above the earth. He has removed our sins as far from us as the east is from the west.

Psalm 103:10-12 NLT

DAY 18

I just feel...

GUILTY FOR SPENDING/EATING/ DRINKING TOO MUCH

My Child,

I know your heart and I know the things that draw you away from me and toward lesser pleasures. Self-hatred accomplishes nothing, except to pull you downward into the spiral of addiction and internal torment. I came to free you from the never-ending cycle of abstinence and indulgence. I want to show you a better way.

Your good behavior does not impress me, just as your bad behavior does not make me angry at you. Every minute of every day I look on you with joy and pride. I am not waiting to punish you for your mistakes; I have already forgiven every wrong decision from yesterday, today and tomorrow.

Legalism is trying to be good apart from my empowering presence; license is abandoning my love to gratify your own needs in destructive ways. Both lead to misery. When My loving acceptance is rooted deep in the soil of your being, you will stop swinging from legalism to license. Bask in the pleasure of knowing you are gloriously loved and all lesser pleasures will be put in their proper order.

You will make known to me the path of life; In Your presence is fullness of joy; In Your right hand there are pleasures forever.

Psalm 16:11 NASB

And because you belong to him, the power of the life-giving Spirit has freed you from the power of sin that leads to death.

Romans 8:2 NLT

DAY 19

I just feel...

TOO LAZY TO PRAY

My Child,

When you put heavy expectations around your relationship with Me, it makes talking with me feel like a chore. I am not looking for fancy language or posture or pretense; I only want to encourage you in the deep places where no one else can reach.

I am always waiting for you, and I know all of the emotional weight you are carrying. I know where you feel disappointed and why you're pushing Me away. I am continuing to pursue your heart and will never stop fighting for you.

There are voices telling you that I am holding out on you, that if I really loved you things would be going better in your life. I am your life. I am your advocate. Just say exactly what you think and feel without filtering it. When you come to Me with raw honesty, I will lift the fog of complacency, energizing you once again with my love.

Jesus answered, "I am the way and the truth and the life. No one comes to the Father except through me.

John 14:6 NIV

All sunshine and sovereign is God, generous in gifts and glory. He doesn't scrimp with his traveling companions.

Psalm 84:11 MSG

DAY 20

I just feel...

LIKE I CARE TOO MUCH ABOUT WHAT OTHER PEOPLE THINK OF ME

My Child,

Your need for love and approval is not a weakness; it is wired into the very nature of your being. You were made for unbroken intimacy, and self-consciousness is a close cousin to shame; it is yet another dark feeling I came to eradicate.

I know you have been criticized, rejected and devastated when you have brought your need for approval to other people who are unacquainted with My love. Those who do not know Me well have a scarcity mentality; they are deceived into thinking their approval can only be won by pulling you down.

I don't want you to become calloused to the opinions of others, but neither do I want you to let their opinions cause you to question your value. As you grow in My loving acceptance, you will figure out which opinions to keep and which to discard.

When you step out in faith, you will experience the feeling of being vulnerable and exposed, but don't take that as a sign to shrink back and lose confidence. You may not have a cheering section on Earth, but you have one in the spirit realm. You are a bold and courageous warrior, fiercely loved and called to greatness!

Keep on being brave! It will bring you great rewards.
Hebrews 10:35 CEV

Obviously, I'm not trying to win the approval of people, but of God. If pleasing people were my goal, I would not be Christ's servant.
Galatians 1:10 NLT

DAY 21

I just feel...

DEPRESSED

My Child,

Hope is your birthright. When your spiritual eyes were opened and you believed, you were given the key to unlock the prison cell of hopelessness. This does not mean you will not encounter seasons of grief. When you experience loss of any kind, I surround you with compassion and mercy. I move heaven and earth to help you rest and recover.

Depression is not a sign that you are broken; it is a sign that the world you live in is broken, and one day I will restore it all. While you wait, take heart that I am on your side. I am right there walking with you through every gripping fear, every heartbreak, every illness. Ignore the shaming voices telling you that your faith is weak or you're not doing enough; this is a time to take solace in only the most compassionate of friends.

Many forces fight against you, but I have overcome them all. One of the most powerful ways to be encouraged is with a song. Even when you can't sing or pray, you can play music that reminds you of My love.

I am never angry with you for feeling depressed. I long to restore your hope; to remind you that better days are ahead. I have such amazing things for you in the future! You have only scratched the surface of experiencing My goodness toward you.

I have told you these things, so that in me you may have peace. In this world you will have trouble. But take heart! I have overcome the world.

John 16:33 NIV

Can a mother forget her nursing child? Can she feel no love for the child she has borne? But even if that were possible, I would not forget you!

Isaiah 49:15 NLT

DAY 22

I just feel...

LIKE MY MIND IS SPINNING

My Child,

Breathe. The pressure is off. Stop and remember that I am right here, and you don't have to figure it all out. The deepest needs you have are already met in My love. I am constantly watching over you. There is nothing to prove, no one to compete with, no advantage you need to get ahead. The world pressures you to produce, but I invite you to abide.

When you feel overwhelmed with your to-do list, ask Me for a higher perspective and I will give it to you. Your mind needs time to roam and to rest; do not overburden it with information you can do nothing about.

My presence is the antidote to all forms of anxiety and fear. All frantic activity ceases when I enter the scene. I long to quiet your mind and stabilize your soul with my love.

Perfectionism is the enemy of peace; release the outcome of each day to me and watch me infuse joy into even the smallest moments.

I have told you these things so that you will be filled with my joy. Yes, your joy will overflow!

John 15:11 NLT

I am leaving you with a gift—peace of mind and heart. And the peace I give is a gift the world cannot give. So don't be troubled or afraid.

John 14:27 NLT

DAY 23

I just feel...
JEALOUS

My Child,

There is more than enough of My goodness to go around. I have not forgotten about you; in time, all of your deepest desires will be met. If there is something you see in another person that you lack, it is only because their path is different from yours. I have given you exactly what you need for this time and season; I am not holding out on you.

I understand it can be painful to see others getting the relationships, opportunities or possessions you want so badly. Say it out loud; take ownership of the feelings, and I will lift your eyes to see the truth of My love.

You are a priceless treasure to me. I have called you to run your race well; do not turn to the left or right but stay focused on My pleasure toward you. Envy will weigh you down and block your joy, and I came that you might have ease and lightness in the core of your being.

Since we are surrounded by so many examples [of faith], we must get rid of *everything* that slows us down, especially sin that *distracts* us. We must run the race that lies ahead of *us* and *never* give up.
Hebrews 12:1 GW

DAY 24

I just feel...

TIRED OF WAITING FOR THINGS TO CHANGE

My Child,

I am a God who wastes nothing. Waiting is a form of suffering, and in every moment of your suffering I am doing something miraculous in you. You cannot see it, but I am knitting your heart to mine, drawing you closer in loving dependence on Me.

I understand your intense frustration; I know it feels as if I am going against My character to not give you what you most desire at this time. Trust that My wisdom is greater, and in the end, your suffering will be transformed into deep, abiding joy.

Where have worn yourself out trying to find a solution, I long to put your soul at ease. You live in a world that wants quick answers, but the deeper work I do takes time. Allow Me to give you grace to endure with a hopeful expectancy. Do not quit! I will help you hang on when you just want to give up. My promises will come to pass, and when the waiting is over you will be so amazed at how you've grown!

And after you have suffered a little while, the God of all grace, who has called you to his eternal glory in Christ, will Himself restore, confirm, strengthen, and establish you.

1 Peter 5:10 ESV

For those God foreknew he also predestined to be conformed to the image of his Son...

Romans 8:29 NIV

DAY 25

I just feel...

REJECTED

My Child,

Imagine standing on the edge of a cliff. Taking a risk in a relationship feels like jumping off into the abyss. What you must realize is that My love is the safety harness. No matter where you jump, you are always safe with Me. I will plant your feet on steady ground. My acceptance of you is final and complete; no one can take it from you. Your identity as My beloved will give you the courage to keep risking even when you face rejection.

Remember that I too experienced deep rejection from those I loved most; I relate with your pain and I want to comfort you.

Rejection cannot derail your destiny. My good plans for you will prevail, despite what you see in your present reality. Do not throw in the towel or stop moving forward.

Let go of bitterness and embrace the truth that I will use every moment of suffering to bring you right where you need to be.

To the praise of the glory of His grace, by which He made us accepted in the Beloved.

Ephesians 1:6 NKJV

The stone that the builders rejected has now become the cornerstone.

Psalm 118:22 NLT

DAY 26

I just feel...

TRAPPED

My Child,

The situations that are making you feel caged in are the very things I am using to turn your attention to my sufficiency. When you cannot see a way out of a difficult circumstance, I am inviting you once again to trust my wisdom. Human decisions made out of fear and pressure will only make things worse. You are looking for relief, but I want you to allow things buried in your heart to surface that I might heal them.

I understand that it seems like things will never change, but I promise they will. Things are changing constantly, and although you feel powerless, I have given you my Spirit that you might respond graciously in this season. When you lose your temper and lash out, I am standing by, ready to forgive.

Relinquish your expectations. Surrender your tight-fisted grip on having things your way. This is a time to dive deeply into my Word and apply the medicine of My promises like balm to a wound. I will bring you through, and once again you will find yourself in a wide open field of freedom.

The Messiah has set us free so that we may enjoy the benefits of freedom. So keep on standing firm in it...
Galatians 5:1 ISV

For God has not given us a spirit of fearfulness, but one of power, love, and sound judgment.
2 Timothy 1:7 HCSB

DAY 27

I just feel...

LIKE NOTHING GOOD CAN COME OUT OF THIS SITUATION

My Child,

Where you see limitations, I see possibilities; where you see an end, I see a new beginning ahead. My creativity shines brightest in the dark places of your life. The dead hopes and dreams you consider worthy of the trash pile become the raw materials I use to create My next masterpiece.

Consider a forest fire: although there is great damage, it is the only way to clear away brush so that sunlight might reach the forest floor and encourage new growth. Do you see it, My child? My love is making way for a gorgeous new grove of fruit-bearing trees.

When your mind wants to go to the worst case scenario, I will buffer your fear with my presence. I understand your pain in letting go of things you hold dear, but beauty and hope are rising where you least expect it! I take delight in surprising my children with gifts. You will shake your head in wonder when you see how I will turn this around for good!

―

And we know that God causes everything to work together for the good of those who love God and are called according to his purpose for them.

Romans 8:28 NLT

DAY 28

I just feel...

OVERWHELMED WITH LUST FOR SOMETHING/SOMEONE I CAN'T HAVE

My Child,

Desire is like a pilot light in your soul—it is always on, but it can be fanned into a roaring flame by the objects of your mind's fascination. You are made in my image, and I am a God of deep passion and desire. I do not command you to stifle your desire, as some have told you; neither do I lead you into a place where desire causes you to self-destruct.

You were created to worship, and lust is worship gone awry. All good and holy desires have been corrupted by humanity, but if you bring Me your raw longings, I will satisfy you in the deepest caverns of your hungry heart. You were made to know and be known. Sometimes strong feelings of lust are a signal that you are hiding your truest self from Me and from your loved ones.

Do not be ashamed to tell Me what you really desire, or that you are angry for not having what you want. I will never condemn you for your soul's hunger; I will do just the opposite and remind you how precious you are to Me.

When you turn to me in honesty and gratitude, you will find your desires fulfilled in ways that are nourishing and life-giving, both for you and for the ones you love the most.

For the world offers only a craving for physical pleasure, a craving for everything we see, and pride in our achievements and possessions. These are not from the Father, but are from this world.

1 John 2:16 NLT

Take delight in the LORD, and he will give you the desires of your heart.

Psalm 37:4 NIV

DAY 29

I just feel...

DISILLUSIONED WITH THE CHURCH

My Child,

My heart is in Spirit-inspired connections, not in man-made institutions. My tribe cannot be contained in a building; My children collectively make up the powerful entity I have chosen to advance My saving work in the world.

Many people in the institution of The Church are unacquainted with My character and My love. I understand the deep disappointment you have faced when encountering hypocrisy, rejection, pettiness and pride in those who claim to know Me. I have seen every incident and I am at work healing your wounds.

Just as I have empowered you to apply mercy and grace with your family members, so it is with the household of faith. I have so much good and meaningful work for you to do; do not allow yourself to pull away and isolate when people rub you the wrong way. Keep your spiritual eyes open, and I will help you find the community where you are both needed and celebrated!

And let us not neglect our meeting together, as some people do, but encourage one another, especially now that the day of his return is drawing near.

Hebrews 10:25 NLT

DAY 30

I just feel...

DISCONTENTED

My Child,

Gratitude is the only exit door out of the dungeon of discontent. That empty, nagging restlessness you feel is only a lack of perspective. You live in a world that encourages discontent in order that you might be easier to manipulate. I have come to center and ground you in the simplicity of My love.

You have everything you need at this moment to be completely content with your life. More money, status, accomplishments or possessions will not make you happier, despite how bombarded you are with messages to the contrary.

My most contented children often have the least worldly status. Cultivate joy by turning off the voices which fuel your discontent. Ask Me to open your eyes to the wonders around you: the laughter of a child, sunlight sparkling off the water, a captivating melody or the kindness of a stranger. My glory surrounds you on every side! Let all striving cease, and breathe in my perfect satisfaction over your entire being. You are complete in Me.

So if we have enough food and clothing, let us be content.
1 Tim 6:8 NLT

In any and all circumstances I have learned the secret of being content—whether well fed or hungry, whether in abundance or in need.
Philippians 4:12 CSB

Day 31

I just feel...

SICKENED BY THE INJUSTICE I SEE IN THE WORLD

My Child,

The opposite of love is not hate; the opposite of love is indifference, and because I *am love*, I am incapable of indifference. I have been accused of being indifferent to suffering, and many have rejected Me because of the dark conditions of this world.

I created man and woman out of the Trinitarian swirl of perfect love, longing for them to partake in its beauty and delight; they were made in My image to love and be loved. However, love demands freedom. I refused to create humans who were forced to love and serve Me, and so I gave them free will. Sin and disobedience was an option as a result of this freedom, and humans have rejected my love and chosen the path of self-sufficiency and pride from the beginning of time until this present day.

My heart bleeds over the consequences of sin, and the only reason I can tolerate it is because I see the end from the beginning. A day is coming when I will right all the wrongs of this created world gone awry.

Do not fret when you see what looks like people getting away with sin. I have witnessed every act of abuse, oppression, evil and injustice, and I will vindicate My beloved children! When you are upset by the evil surrounding you, remember that light always dispels darkness. Turn your eyes to Me and let your fear and anguish be turned to peace and tranquility as you trust My timing in setting all things right.

I saw heaven standing open and there before me was a white horse, whose rider is called Faithful and True. With justice he judges and wages war. His eyes are like blazing fire, and on his head are many crowns. He has a name written on him that no one knows but he himself…Coming out of his mouth is a sharp sword with which to strike down the nations. 'He will rule them with an iron scepter.' He treads the winepress of the fury of the wrath of God Almighty. On his robe and on his thigh he has this name written: KING OF KINGS AND LORD OF LORDS.
Revelation 19:11-16 NIV

About the Author

Rebekah McLeod is a freelance writer, musician, and storyteller. She spent seven years as an independent singer/songwriter, releasing two albums and touring regionally in the Washington, D.C. Metro area. After blogging for three years, Rebekah published a book, *The Secret Life of a Doctor's Wife*, in 2016. She is currently a ghostwriter, writing coach and co-founder of Marigold Press Books Publishing Company. Her children's book, *The Hungry Sun*, was released in December 2022.

MARIGOLD PRESS BOOKS

Relationship focused, independent publisher sharing stories of hope.

Marigold Press Books was created to build a legacy by sharing stories of hope and magnifying the voices of women. Founders Emra Smith and Rebekah McLeod saw a gap in the industry that left budding authors wandering and aimless. Their intention is to provide a relationship focused publishing experience where they guide authors through the entire process from idea inception to published book to marketing and more.

Visit Us
www.marigoldpressbooks.org

Instagram
@marigoldpressbooks

Email
marigoldpressbooks@gmail.com